# EMerging from DRead

# EMerging from DRead

Poems by

Noralyn Masselink

Kelsay Books

© 2016 Noralyn Masselink. All rights reserved. This material may not be reproduced in any form, published, reprinted, recorded, performed, broadcast, rewritten or redistributed without the explicit permission of Noralyn Masselink. All such actions are strictly prohibited by law.

ISBN 13- 978-1-945752-20-9

*Kelsay Books*
Alabaster Leaves Publishing
www.kelsaybooks.com

*To the One without whom
these poems would never have been written*

# Acknowledgments

While all glory goes to God, I am deeply indebted and will forever be grateful to Adiel Gonzalez, the nurse midwife and first reader of these poems. You not only *told* me you could help me when my world was falling down around me, but you actually stuck by me long enough to do it—and to help me rebuild a better world. Thank you for teaching me to be "selfish in a good way" and that it is o.k. to be Too Much. Thank you also for being my friend.

Sincere thanks go out to those who read and re-read my poems, encouraging me all the way, most notably Vicki Boynton, Lori O'Donnell, Alex Gonzalez, and (especially) my daughter Emmalon Davis, who also contributed photos for the cover art.

I also want to thank my prayer partner, Mary Pettit, who faithfully prayed that my writing would find favor, and O.P.W. Fredericks, Editor of The Lives You Touch Press, who encouraged me to submit my poems to Kelsay Books.

While it might seem odd for me to thank my ex-husband, I do. If love is stronger than death, it can also be stronger than divorce and everything that leads to divorce. Thank you for the good times and for the three beautiful daughters we share.

And finally, I want to thank all three of my daughters for loving me and forgiving me for my parenting failures. Just never forget that God redeems what the locusts have eaten and turns our mourning into dancing. Yes, He does exceedingly abundantly beyond all we can ask or imagine.

An early, untitled version of "Prowess" appeared in *Fishfood Literary and Creative Arts Magazine* (November 15, 2014), and "Garage Cleanout" appeared in *The Riveter Review* 5 (August 2016).

# Contents

## IMAGE

| | |
|---|---|
| Photo: | 15 |
| The Rift | 16 |
| Stripped Ease | 17 |
| Wrong | 18 |
| Of *course*, I can't sing | 19 |
| From Merest Threat | 20 |
| A Glass of Wine Too Much | 21 |

## BONDAGE

| | |
|---|---|
| First Car | 25 |
| Mr. Fix-It | 26 |
| Freudian Error | 27 |
| Pseudonym | 28 |
| Thanksgiving Day 1988 | 30 |
| Forced Family Unity | 31 |
| Ode to D.K., His Psychiatrist | 32 |

## BREAKAGE

| | |
|---|---|
| Ratios | 35 |
| Pipe Dreams | 36 |
| Prowess | 37 |
| All Ways | 39 |
| In Retrospect | 40 |
| Recipe for Dead Woman Dessert | 41 |
| A Valediction: Requiring Mourning | 42 |

## TRIAGE

| | |
|---|---:|
| The Nurse Midwife | 45 |
| EMDR Therapy Session 1 | 46 |
| EMDR Therapy Session 2 | 47 |
| Place | 48 |
| EMDR Therapy Session 3 | 49 |
| Dissimilitude | 51 |
| Active Inertia | 52 |

## CLEAVAGE

| | |
|---|---:|
| Deviation | 55 |
| Final Concession | 56 |
| Anomie | 58 |
| Double-edged | 59 |
| ICU | 60 |
| Complicated Grieving | 61 |
| The Naturalistic Fallacy | 63 |

## SEEPAGE

| | |
|---|---:|
| Stuff | 67 |
| PTSD | 68 |
| Narcotic Succor | 69 |
| Night Terrors | 70 |
| EMDR Therapy Session 4 | 71 |
| In need of GPS: Grace, Poise, Serenity | 72 |
| Retreat to Silence | 73 |

## PASSAGE

| | |
|---|---|
| EMDR Therapy Session 5 | 77 |
| The Therapist Listens | 78 |
| Aftermath | 79 |
| Reciprocity | 80 |
| EMDR Therapy Session 6: Propinquity | 81 |
| Loose Ends | 82 |
| Little Red Wagon | 83 |

## BRICOLAGE

| | |
|---|---|
| The Swimming Pool | 87 |
| Garage Cleanout | 88 |
| Dragon Fly | 89 |
| Silence | 90 |
| The Other Shoe | 91 |
| Renovation | 92 |
| EMDR Therapy Session 7 | 93 |

## AFTERIMAGE

| | |
|---|---|
| Unexpected Take-Off | 97 |
| Selective Hearing | 98 |
| *I can help you* | 100 |
| A Book Proposal | 101 |
| Today's Special | 102 |
| Unmolested | 103 |
| Garudasana | 104 |

About the Author

IMAGE

# Photo:

alone on new year's eve—Singapore
sling of cruel reality
sad girl
the one you sang about
but could not bear to see

# The Rift

*You deserve good things!*

good things given lavished bestowed
luxurious plenteous tasteful sweet
for young girls (and old) they do get weary
and tenderness a little tenderness
will chase away the nasty face
indeed she's waiting, anticipating
things he'll never ever possess
so sentimental those soft words spoken
made rage easier to bear yeah

she regrets her grief and care
but can't forget that love
was her whole happiness
though he forgot the ending
or perhaps he never knew
(or knew and used it to subdue)
that never leave her
*is* the tender
happiness she grieves

## Stripped Ease

young fit tall slim
she stands in silk
seductive
dressed not to kill
perhaps to die
not wishing to be murdered
but stabbed she was
and more than once
though all her moves
designed for him ignoring
wrists first sore then numb
and his assuming she had come
lips swollen nearly raw
his (s)word deadly rejection

# Wrong

something's off
you sense a vibe
which I must
too
now recognize
to know how I went

Wrong

did I delay in my response?
raise my voice?
snatch?

Wrong

but once I
figure out what's
Wrong
then it's my job
to make it right

kiss?
give you space?
make a banana pie?

Wrong

you will not say—
this too
I must now
figure out,
magically through ESP
must see how I am

Wrong

# Of *course,* I can't sing

God forbid
that I should sing
can't do that
'cause that is yours

just like anger
that's yours too

what's mine is yours
what's yours is yours
and what was ours
is now yours too

and what you tell me
that's what goes

and everything
depends on you

# From Merest Threat

from
merest
thread
to
one-inch
cable
reinforced
through
many
years
from
throat to
groin
steel
spiral
rigid
in
ex
or
able

# A Glass of Wine Too Much

Cabernet kiss
shell-less snail
stranded starfish
nursing sow

no wonder
layered scales
become a second skin
elbow-length gloves
50's movie
elegant veneer
to cover
lacerations

# BONDAGE

# First Car

purchased at twenty-something
with my life's savings
make, model, even color
all forgotten
but I can still see clearly
rushing from his rage
to the protection of its locks
believing (blind naiveté)
that a vehicle could carry me to safety
but he who stripped my cables
kept me trapped
in his control
unable for some twenty-something years
to drive away

# Mr. Fix-It

you knew to put cardboard over holes in shoes
a wiz with duct tape
the crazy glue king
could jimmy-rig a broken fridge
there seemed no fixing you couldn't do

you sewed in crotches of torn-out pants
patched screens, rebuilt sockets, pool pumps, lamps
but one thing always
you neglected
to repair

the damaged
scrambled
mangled
you

# Freudian Error

my father was a gentle man
with advanced degrees
and quiet ways
and hands that polished little girl patent leathers
and cleaned my mother's kitchen floors

my husband was a gentle man, too
with few degrees
and a song-bird's voice
and hands that tied his daughters' shoes
and buffed and waxed my hardwood floors

two gentlemen
with gentle ways
abruptly erupting
sweet peace interrupting
corrupted by ignoble rage

# Pseudonym

I told her
my name is Theresa
an outright lie
pulled from the thin air
that had had me
gasping for breath
for weeks
in this shiny new city of mine

she told me
*look for the porch*
*with the blue light on*
why blue, I thought
why not red
to better reflect the danger, dismay
the five-bell alarm
catapulting me to her phone-line

and when
I found my way to her June porch
(heart fibrillating,
infant so-so safe
within the Snugli on my chest)
I found no words to share
why I had come
dared not expose myself

beyond the fact
that I had called
and I had come
and I was sitting on her porch
unable to speak the words

that would have made
what could not be
reality

could not even say my name
certainly could not tell
that I'd arrived
carried by my Ph.D.
could not detail the facts that made
me just one more of the one in four
stupid enough
to be abused

# Thanksgiving Day 1988

thank God for heat
and (her) paycheck
to cover their electric bill
so he (who does not work)
can sit in comfort
no matter that it's cold outside
and these old windows leak
his right to sit with no clothes on
trumps hers to steward heat

when she so stupid carefully
has the dumb audacity
to ask if putting on a sweater might not help?
and then as if that weren't enough,
has the boldfaced nerve to touch the dial
wrong move, wrong move (way, way, *way* off)—
she's stripped him of his power
kicked him in the balls

*fuck you*s flung out
rampage and smash
makes sure she sees
her place
who's boss
and who's in charge
of what can be enjoyed

but after 911 is called
when all is calm
though not so bright
they carry on again
oh yeah—
and happy holiday!

# Forced Family Unity

you called it FFU
an acronym reminding
me of profanity
curse words you clung to
equated with who you
(incomprehensible to me)
insisted you were—
a nigger—
even telling an acquaintance
(as I discovered decades later)
much to her amazement
that black kids *need* the belt

of course,
our time together
should have been
for fun
for play
and not a chore
required
a prescription

what made what other people do—
picnics, board games,
sitting on sofas in *family* rooms—
so impossible for us
incumbent together
on our hard futon
in a wrecked room?

# Ode to D.K., His Psychiatrist

Once upon a time a scared young woman came to you, hopes and dreams and husband in tow frightened, dismayed, dismantled: "My husband's threatened to burn our house down." And the highly paid psychiatrist said, "I recommend the book *Let the Dog Drive.*"

Scared young woman came back again, hopes and dreams, husband, and baby girl in tow confused, disoriented, discouraged: "Here are definitions of violence and abuse; I think that's what's going on." And the highly paid family psychiatrist said, "Keep it crazy. Make sure he has creative outlets, a safe place to let off steam."

Scared (not so) young woman appeared again, hopes and dreams, husband, and two young girls in tow desperate, demoralized, discomposed: "Should I check myself in to a shelter for battered women?" And the highly paid well-known family psychiatrist said, "His bark is worse than his bite; you should do what you do best."

Stuck middle-aged woman returned, hopes and dreams, husband, and three young girls in tow resigned, dissociated, distressed: "Our fifteen-year old put a knife in her backpack to defend herself against her father." And the highly paid well-known family psychiatrist said, "Are you concerned that he does not love her as much as you?"

And so, the woman let the dog drive, and the husband stayed safe by leaving periodically, which meant that life was always crazy, and though the husband usually only barked (telling her, among other things, that he had fantasies of slitting her throat), sometimes he bit too (pushed, slapped, and shook or held her against her will), but the woman did what she knew best and the girls they coped as they knew how, and happily ever after never came, but hey, the psychiatrist got paid.

# BREAKAGE

# Ratios

from 30:70 to the reverse
ratio measuring pleasure to pain
mathematical proof suggesting to her
in two point four decades a solid net gain

so proud of that progress from obscene to decent
from ferociously bad to passably good
and assuming the same steady rate of progression
(aware what "assume" makes of you and of me)
she figures perhaps that in forty years maybe
things might be (maybe) just as they should
with no slaps or rages and no separations
100:0 (unless she is dead)

# Pipe Dreams

die harder than adamantine rock
and like an electro-magnet
reclaiming scraps from a rubbish heap
attract the derelict heart

stripped
scourged
beaten
bare

sacrificed
beyond recovery
no repair

# Prowess

leave me once shame on you
leave me twice shame on me
what happens when
you leave me three
and four and five
or six and seven?
shame swells distends and octuplies
guilt, fault, regret infuse my bones
form infrastructure of their own
rigid, inflexible as steel
devastating marrow

each time I reason, scrape, pray, cry
plead, grovel, and cajole
till weeping begging
yield
concede
exhausted acquiesce

then when shame has paralyzed
when leaving's past
grand exit over
when grief has numbed
and anesthesia grips
you swoop back in
intensive care
reviving dreams from death-grip snare
your scalpel skilled
debulks my soul
your chemo love kills more than hair
roots zapped by radiation

and you restore what you destroyed
rehabbing long and slow
till I've survived ten fifteen years
perfecting your defection

# All Ways

always threaten
threaten to abandon
abandon me never
never let me
let me go

# In Retrospect

*It's a good life if you don't fold*
a strange motto for you to hold
since (each time the stakes were high)
you laid down your cards
like the pleated napkins
my mother insisted be reused
from meal to meal
expecting us to take up
and work around
last night's debris
to wipe this morning's lips

# Recipe for Dead Woman Dessert
(Calls for ingredients readily at hand)


Prepare one gaping hole in ground.
Pour in concrete vault.
Layer lumps of self in brass-trimmed coffin.
Wrap in formaldehyde fondant (fear works just as well).
Top with marble monument.
Sprinkle generously with dirt.

Serves one self-serving husband well.

Note: concoction keeps indefinitely;
the topping is key, don't skimp on that.

# A Valediction: Requiring Mourning

three golden strands to airy thinness beat

so fixed on hope and joy and love was she
that other strings entangled, beaten in
she quite ignored—

the leaden ropes of silencing and stricture
brass cables of resentment, ultimatums, fear
iron wires of being left, rejected, scorned—

encumbered hope joy love across the years
till beaten into earth
her golden strands now lie—junkyard alloy

# TRIAGE

# The Nurse Midwife

star of David on his neck
more gypsy than clinician
for weeks I wondered what he was

Mnemosyne his mother,
his gift?
to care, bear memories—

an Orpheus
with new songs to sing
in a clearer higher key

how does it work?
this miracle he summons
transposing pain to poetry

he will say
*it isn't me;*
*the client leads, controls*

but having failed myself
I fear that
I will fail him too

still, I promise to persist
make pearls from parasites
and grit

# EMDR* Therapy Session 1

Therapy Session 1

two fingers     to and fro

pressing     passing
probing     pulling

    consumed by how long it is taking, his tiring arm
    thinking ever of the other    unable to let go

*Follow my fingers*
    so she does--trying too hard to let go
    ever mindful, always mindful of her frown
    her spastic fingers, clenching toes, and urge to heave
        penetralia offered   paraded out  in plainest view
    mile-wide eyes, infant cries
    testify to what she's been denied

*Go to your safe place*

---

*Developed by Francine Shapiro, Ph.D., EMDR (Eye Movement Desensitization and Reprocessing) is a powerful psychotherapy treatment which alleviates the emotional distress associated with disturbing events and helps clients replace negative thoughts and perceptions with more adaptive responses.

# EMDR Therapy Session 2

*place your feet
flat on the floor—
it's protocol*, he says
(one's heels are spades
to dig up dirt
decades of buried rage)

and when the session is complete
her eyes still hanging down

she sees dark marks from her own shoes
have shouted, screamed her shame
black slashes scuffed her polished floor
soul gashes, flashes from her past
materialized without consent
as feet relived her pain

# Place

*Go* to what? Go
*to* where? to
*your*
*safe* what? where safe?
*place*

# EMDR Therapy Session 3

feet tensed on a chair rung, her body shrinks away
his maleness much too close too near to horror

*Because*   you   *deserve good things*
her hand goes up       her face averts
her thoughts construct the unseen wall
**Don't** say that, she directs, her anger piling high

his words like slugs in a coin slot
jam    do not compute
fly disintegrate implode self-destruct in air

*Put your feet down on the floor* [can cement turn into clay?]
*Relax* [prepare to cast yourself out into tainted space]
*Look at my fingers* [be glad it's not his face]

eyes try hard to keep her secrets—barely open following
instantly they pull away—too much too much way way too much
          waywaywayway   too much

*Just keep following my fingers* [there's nothing just about it]

## You were in my face            How could that be so?

I'm glad you thought you'd killed me glad you felt some fear
I felt nothing eyes rolled back in shock without a tear
only later whiplash pain that followed through the years
telling me to keep my place though where impossible to say

## Get up       you pull me up and lead me down
          as in control in this as when you made me

                                        f
                                          all

and I have not forgotten in the twenty years that passed the only things I'm missing are the reasons you harassed and what I said did didn't do to end up on the floor and in this chair with arms crossed tight and woe-filled cries hating her hating her hating her hating her hating her hated by him

Poor little girl who loved unwisely and not well
                                                                                    who fell
                        for soul decimation
                                                                                      not soul mate

# Dissimilitude

*Like a miscarriage?*
he'd asked,
trying to understand
what had passed
at our last session

no, not at all like a miscarriage
nothing spontaneous or natural
about this post-due travail
my contractions useless
for delivering
this crude-ball fetus

so much more than Pitocin,
your forceps required
to drag out this stillborn
(a bogey gestation)
preventing
fistula abscess
maternal death

# Active Inertia

her tears are dirty
like the bathwater
which, though nearly scalding
when she'd first stepped in,
grew tepid
as
convulsed in pain
nose plugged
again
face blotched
again
each time the same
again
an old refrain

till finally
the cold
contempt
like stones thrown
at a home-grown prophet
envelop her,
shuddering
alone
forlorn
in her tub

# CLEAVAGE

# Deviation*

two roads diverged no yellow wood
(not sorry at all she could not travel both)
she'd walked the one less traveled by
and that had made the difference

now ages and ages hence
she tells with a sigh
of leaves her steps had trodden black
long rotten, not forgotten

and how much further down that road
the road diverged again
one way leading on towards dreamt of goal
and well she knew where that bend led

and what the undergrowth would bring
as way led unto way

and though she'd been so certain when
she'd first chosen that way
had certainly not marked the other for another day
another day had come and now

two roads diverged again
and as one traveler standing there
she must choose now
the road not taken then

*with thanks, of course, to Robert Frost

# Final Concession

he could
        had
                did
                        was
                              in control
all that she had she'd offered
he stayed? she paid
he left? she paid
she paid
        and paid
                and paid
                        and paid

but now I've filed for divorce
half that I have I've offered
and so I wait
wait for a call
or wait for no response at all

he can
        has
                does
                      is
                          in control
he takes? I pay
he leaves? I pay
I pay
    and pay
            and pay
                    and pay
this one last time
so from now on

I can
    have
        do
            and will be
                    in control

# Anomie

*If you got what you deserved,
you would not be alive*

his statement typical
(i.e., threatening, bizarre)
though in this case a non-sequitur
since all she'd asked
was why *he'd* asked
her to withdraw
her action for divorce

# Double-edged

(s)words (s)lash her (he)art
(d)anger (d)wells in the (per)severance
lightning (st)rips through black (ter)rain
(end)less (dis)comfort in her (dis)stress
(d)riven she (r)ends her own (dis)quiet
(un)easy her new (circum)stance

# ICU

*you walked ten miles in,* this friend had said
*now you must walk ten out*
twenty-four years of striding into snarly woods
had brought me to that moment of collapse
tangled despair

the "back out" part, she had that right
the distance too, correct
but mangled, torn, I could not walk
or crawl
needed to be hauled
at least the first few miles

no one expects a legless man to walk out of the woods
till he receives prosthetic parts
all he can do is shout
use his arms to drag himself along
pray he won't pass out
or be devoured by wild animals

so I
who wanted nothing more
than the forest floor to swallow me
could not envision traveling an inch
forget about a mile

still, her words to my wounds
were a tourniquet
arresting shock
enabling me
to resist death
for one more hour

her care had carried me

# Complicated Grieving

you say you've lost a loved one?
lucky you
be glad
no restrictions to your sorrow
woe is you and wail away
do not eat,
or binge all day
weep in the shower
beat your bed

simple grief
straight way ahead
no retrieval from the dead
you can long with all you have
wish and hope or dream and pray
and though heart bending, stomach rending
simple grief is impotent
to change what death destroys

not so when grief is mixed with fear
when what she grieves
is alive, still here
merely a quick phone call away
phone call that brings back disarray
(undoes what eight long months have done
to pull her from the grave)
phone call that resurrects him
to her life
but locks her in a coffin

such grief not safe
not to be savored

must be snuffed out or set aside
lest she be weak and call to life
that which will kill
and thereby doom
to everlasting sorrow
what's just begun to live in me

# The Naturalistic Fallacy

he'd called,
the estranged husband
asking her to meet
and she
knowing
but breaking
all the rules
agreed

the public place
the scenic lake
assuaging
dampening
memories
of kohl blue eyes
hand printed cheeks
orders of protection

it was all over
the news reports
young mother of four
strangled and drowned
in Stewart Park
shaded lakeside retreat
for families like hers
will no longer be

but over beers
his friends agreed
she'd had it coming
those kids were his
not hers to take away

and so he'd shown
her who was boss
which she should just have known

# SEEPAGE

# Stuff

Old stuff
Tough stuff
Old tough stuff
Stuff old tough stuff

# PTSD

flash forwards flood
my basement stairs
(mud colored to best hide the dirt)

recurring visions intimate
a face-first hurtle—
sequel to the backward drag

fresh rug burn blood
staining umber carpet
shading the ghosts of former scabs

# Narcotic Succor

*looped out on codeine numbness*
line loops meanders through her brain
chardonnay haze
stupor not grief
stupid relief
now seeping through her sleep
night terrors tear her
up
down
keep her
*looped out on codeine numbness*

# Night Terrors

pierce her
sodden sleepless nights
like the keening
of a middle-Eastern widow
projecting anxious certitude
that she'll be left
alone
collecting the effects
of another unseen sniper's eye

# EMDR Therapy Session 4

seconds away from curtains
lights out
black hole
throat scraped sea shell grit raw

his fingers pass but do not touch

attempting to dislodge the skin
stuck
strangling me
in my own dining room

# In need of GPS: Grace, Poise, Serenity

Mr. Elusive well and good
you make me figure for myself
but why? when you're the expert
and I'm lost
what good are you
when all you do is watch me
spin in circles?

you will say that I am free
to pull out of my spin
but what good does such pulling do
when traffic circles loom
and I don't know which loop to take
that won't bring me right back around
to where my trip began?

and you say *don't fight me*
as if I had the energy
and wherewithal
when all I know
is that I'd like to sit a spell
and sip some wine
until my whirling stops

# Retreat to Silence

safe place not secure

but safest space
her silent oasis
my palisade again

# PASSAGE

# EMDR Therapy Session 5

retching on curds of silence
gag order
obstructs
occludes

nothing in, nothing out
only throttling at her throat
years of stifling to surrender
decades of denying darkness

stomach clenching squeeze
constriction
pressure ruptures
primal scream

# The Therapist Listens

ears keenly tuned to sense slight shift in pitch
as whispers disclose covert truths
subjected now
to pulverizing screams
his nearness necessary
insuring she is safe
though lacerated nerves say no

if he
to shield himself from her torment
placed fingers in his ears
she
with eyes squeezed shut
against the horror
would never be the wiser

# Aftermath

all she feels is flat_____

first fetters
waters broken
initial evacuation

she heaves
but reflex swallows hard
keeps bile in

this too will go
not soon enough
but soon

and she will thank her nurse midwife
sitting near through midnight hour
urging but not forcing her

to open up
push out
let go

# Reciprocity

rock  me  hard place
to(o) extreme(s)
hard
to be the one
exposing all
opening fragile ledges  up
to wind and rain
      baring jagged edge
           soft sandstone scrapings
eroding

Newton's third
supposed-to-be a law
so out of reach

so

I rest low
on my rock heap
algae
without fungi
lichen-less

irreciprocity

# EMDR Therapy Session 6: Propinquity

seated diagonally face to face
except my face and eyes are closed
his knee is near (way, way too near)
proximity unspeakable
my face my shoulders shrinking back
I work to unfold, untie myself
from forces drawing me
in dreadlock knots
away from him

and *he* said
*focus on what we did*
but she
now finished
with eyes agape
cannot get past
still marvels at
the closeness of
their chairs

## Loose Ends

stray threads still mar
her tapestry
begging to be picked at, cut, or burnt away

perfectionism demanding
everything be neat
each thread accounted for, nothing stray

and though I've bound the edges
plucked white from black
eliminated gray

again and now
her heart tells me
that I have lost my way

## Little Red Wagon

one wheel's off
her axle's dragging
pretty little pity wagon
painted black
clattering thoughts
in disarray
directionless
circular

yet she knows this

that as she can
she'll sand the black
till red shines through
and fix the axle
dragging down
find a new wheel
to replace the old
order thoughts
in new array
and forge ahead
to her true north

# BRICOLAGE

# The Swimming Pool

Don't cry.
DO
NOT
CRY!
I will myself as tears well up
on the edge
of a 16 x 32 foot in-ground pool
in over my head
the maintenance guy talking breezily of floaters
backwash, stabilizers, earth
more new world for me to rise above
along with intangibles
(like pain and shame and insecurity)
wouldn't it just be easier to shovel dirt
and fill the damn thing in?

this is the life, I used to say
Italian ice melting in the tropical drink
you'd concocted
basking in my plastic boat
savoring the sunny life of the rich and famous
we couldn't quite believe was ours

and now this life is mine
except my boat has sprung
a long, slow leak
and what I drink when I come in
from vacuuming the pool
are tears I swallowed back
instead of sliding down
over the edge
of
in over my head

# Garage Cleanout

*It will pay for itself*
or so he'd claimed
as he'd pressed her into shelling out the dough
for a rebuilt beast of a sit-down mower
only he could manhandle
and she could barely straddle

she had paid his good deal price
in that (as in all things, it seemed)
so now, a world of twelve months later
her grass uncut, the mower sits
collecting dust, rusting in her garage,
a home to nesting mice

# Dragon Fly

why did you choose my window sill
open to a junk-filled garage
you who should have hovered
over sun-splashed ponds
among swaying reeds
or ridden on the back of a mate
as gossamer as you?

I tried to save you set you free
from certain death
in dusty dark captivity
with broomstick long
reached up to tap the sill
to shake you clear

how could I know my tap
would loosen that top pane
in guillotine descent
to sever graceful wings
so fine
but not quite swift enough?

# Silence

her friend
an older sister
strong, secure
not prone to breakdowns or collapse

sturdy like the wood fence
around her in-ground pool
a barrier that in no way
keeps rabbits, moles, or toads
from slipping in
but does prevent
my own insides
from sliding out

# The Other Shoe

you say that I am waiting for the other shoe to drop
why would I not?
having spent a lifetime
dodging an array of falling shoes
with feet inside
aimed squarely at my back

as if like Anderson's naïve fool
I wore a sign
for all to see
inviting anyone who wanted
to *kick me*

but now you've asked me to step out
in Jimmy Choo's
envision sunny skies
or better yet run barefoot

as if I owned my stride
and can direct my path
away from well-worn heels and steel-toed boots

accept as fact the benign row of empty shoes
paired neatly on my closet floor

# Renovation

with a flick of his wrists
to fictive reins
horse whisperer
in reverse

not taming
but helping me recapture
feral fierceness
wilding heart

transmuting
this worn out hack
into a winner-takes-all
star

# EMDR Therapy Session 7

two fingers     to and fro

pressing       passing
probing        pulling

*let it go*
      legion ossified
*old stuff*
      host petrified
*you are safe*
      impossible—yet true

not-so-little death, no breath

                                and finally the letting go

# AFTERIMAGE

# Unexpected Take-Off

last week we talked of the new plane
I'd wheeled into my driveway
and my desire to sit a while
just sit and run my hands
my eyes over strange controls
not have to fly
just revel in safety
buckled on the ground
certainly not take off in a raging storm

but somehow here I am
already in flight
with smoldering clouds and turbulence
ahead of lessons on air thrust
or how to use the throttle

tossed out into midair

but since I did not throw myself
off the highest steeple
do not expect blue angel demonstration
I'll rest secure, rely on autopilot
to catch me though I nose dive

and meanwhile I'm so thankful
for wingman on my rear

# Selective Hearing

what he said was
nothing more
than what they'd said,
this man who sat
while others stood
beside me

then why did what
he said take hold
when their words
slid away?

was it
that he'd seen me nude?
but they had too
though *that* bareness
seems down-right burka draped
compared to strip show
self-disclosure
full exposure
I'd arrayed
for him

or was it
that he'd held my hand
(but they had too)
through child birth pangs
had heard me scream
gyrate in pain
and squeeze my eyes
to shut him out?

or in the end
does all depend
on one Y
having all the power
to trump
a pair of X's?

## *I can help you*

24 years
8 therapists
4 words

oh, others helped,
helped me to cope
do dead woman's float

but only you saw that to save
you'd need to pull
from a saltwater grave

one who'd floundered all her life
nearly drift wood
now on solid ground

# A Book Proposal

six pearls in a plastic bag
the books he'd lent me
on abuse and psychotherapy
jewels in a garland
he'd begun to string
decades ago
to place around my neck
when he walked through my door

and though the titles grate
and the print is small
footnotes complicated
statistics raw
still I will cherish every page
and search for gaps
that I can fill
with pearls of my own

# Today's Special

how very ironic
and what are the chances
on this first birthday of my new single life
that the restaurant special
fresh sandwich I order
is named after the former love of my life
grilled chicken with crab cake and spicy white sauce
delicious
despite its unfortunate name

like removing the stinger
and savoring sweetness
enjoying the honey
after honey bee's death

# Unmolested

shedding
by divine alchemy
more than a skimpy sundress
her wispy cobweb shell of shame
floats above hot concrete
till a flimsy breeze wafts it away
mystifying metamorphosis

butterfly strokes
through her backyard pool
water warm, lean body cool
dolphin kicks thrust naked flow
each stroke full peak achieves

then head laid back with tipsy laugh
a weightless cross, she floats
soft belly up
exposed
this time unscathed
till prune skin fingers
say she's had enough

my heart alive
preserved and free
without a push
assents
agrees

# Garudasana

performance clouded first attempts
concern that I might fail
sadhaka effort
awkward
trying this
and that
to no avail

until

in spaceless time
pranayama found
beyond inadequacy
balance
grace
poise
strength

grounded in flight

# About the Author

Noralyn Masselink is a Professor of English at SUNY-Cortland in central New York, a Pilates and Yoga instructor at the local YWCA, and the mother of three daughters who inspire her regularly. Her poems have appeared in *TWJ Magazine, S/tick, RedFez, RiverLit, The Riveter Review,* and *Fishfood Literary & Creative Arts Magazine.* Her chapbook *Song of My Breast,* a collection recounting the experience of undergoing treatment for invasive breast cancer, was published in spring 2015 by The Lives You Touch Publications. A second chapbook *Once Upon a Rhyme (or Not?)* (also on the topic of domestic violence) was published by the same press in September 2016, and a third chapbook "two-edged (s)word(s)" is forthcoming. Noralyn is intrigued by the power of words (and, above all, the Word) to rein in, rain on, and reign over whatever circumstances are submitted to their discipline.